The Ha-Ha Party

Story by Joy Cowley

The clowns had a ha-ha party
to see who was the funniest.
The prize was a giant clown cake.

"That will be my cake!"
said the pink clown.

"No, my cake!"
said the yellow clown.

"Mine!" the blue clown said.

3

The pink clown said to the judges,
"Do you want to see something funny
Then watch this!"
He pulled a cat out of his hat.

The judges smiled and nodded.

"I am funnier,"
said the yellow clown.
"Watch me!"
She walked on her hands
and juggled a ball with her feet.

The judges nodded,
and the cat went to sleep
on the pink clown's head.

"I'm the funniest,"
said the blue clown.
"Listen to my joke.
What do mice eat
when they go to a party?"

"We don't know,"
said the other clowns.
"What *do* mice eat
when they go to a party?"

8

"Mice? Party?"
Suddenly, the cat was awake.

The cat was on the table
before the blue clown
could say, "Mice cream!"

"Mice? Party? Where?"

The cat ran up and down,
looking under the dishes.

The judges began to laugh.

11

The three clowns
tried to catch the cat.
They fell over the table.
The table crashed to the floor.

The judges laughed and clapped.
"That's very funny!" they cried.
"That gets the prize!"

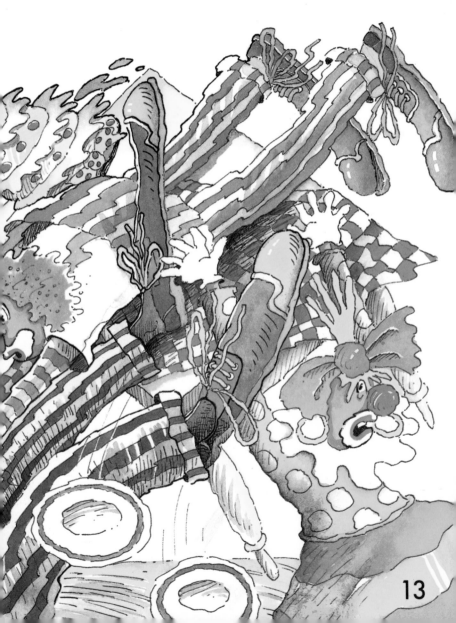

Then the judges said,
"On your own,
you weren't very funny.
But together, you were hilarious.
You should always work together."

"We will," said the clowns,
"and we'll start with this cake."